Editor

Sara Connolly

Editor in Chief

Ina Massler Levin, M.A.

Creative Director

Karen J. Goldfluss, M.S. Ed.

Illustrator

Clint McKnight

Cover Artist

Marilyn Goldberg

Art Coordinator

Renée Mc Elwee

Imaging

James Edward Grace

Publisher

Mary D. Smith, M.S. Ed.

Author

Christine Smith

The classroom teacher may reproduce copies of the materials in this book for use in a single classroom only. The reproduction of any part of the book for other classrooms or for an entire school or school system is strictly prohibited. No part of this publication may be transmitted, stored, or recorded in any form without written permission from the publisher.

Teacher Created Resources

6421 Industry Way
Westminster, CA 92683
www.teachercreated.com

ISBN: 978-1-4206-5907-8

© *2011 Teacher Created Resources*
Made in U.S.A.

Table of Contents

Introduction

The visual puzzles in *Start to Finish: What's Different?* are designed to stimulate thinking skills, support content standards, and entertain students. Each puzzle page presents students with an interesting fact that ties into the classroom curriculum and two pictures to examine. The students are then challenged to look at the pictures carefully and identify what is different.

Visual puzzles that encourage students to identify differences are more than just fun activities. They reinforce and stimulate critical-thinking and problem-solving skills. As students solve the puzzles, they are improving their observation skills and attention to detail. Their brains are learning to evaluate and analyze visual data through comparison. Students can also work on their fine-motor skills and eye-hand coordination by coloring the pictures.

The puzzles in this book can be used in learning centers, as extension activities, for students who finish early, and as at-home enrichment activities. Have fun learning!

Insects Everywhere

Insects can be found all over Earth. Entomologists, scientists who study insects, have named over one million types of insects. That's a lot of bugs!

Look at these pictures. Circle 7 things that are different in the picture above.

Snow Day

Are you hoping for a snow day? Then watch the outside temperature. Water freezes at 32°F. So for snow to form and build up it must be 32°F or below.

Look at these pictures. Circle 7 things that are different in the picture above.

Solar Energy

Light travels from the sun to Earth in about eight minutes. We can use this solar energy to heat water and buildings, grow plants, and make electricity.

Look at these pictures. Circle 7 things that are different in the picture above.

Calories Count

The energy in food is measured in calories. You need food energy to stay healthy, but eating too many calories or not enough calories can be bad for your health.

Look at these pictures. Circle 8 things that are different in the picture above.

Going, Going, Gone

About 1,000 animals are listed as endangered. They need to be protected from environmental changes, disease, and overhunting or they may become extinct.

Look at these pictures. Circle 7 things that are different in the picture above.

Living with Chimpanzees

Would you like to live with chimpanzees? Jane Goodall did. She watched and studied chimpanzees in Gombe National Park in Tanzania for over 20 years.

Look at these pictures. Circle 7 things that are different in the picture above.

Stargazing

The stars do not move. They appear to move because the Earth is always moving. It rotates on its axis once every 24 hours and orbits around the sun once every 365 days.

Look at these pictures. Circle 7 things that are different in the picture above.

Galileo and the Telescope

Galileo Galilei built the first telescope strong enough to study space in 1609. Now we have telescopes that can see billions of light years away.

Look at these pictures. Circle 7 things that are different in the picture above.

Magnetic North

A compass uses the magnetic field of the Earth. The needle of the compass is a magnet. The north end of the needle is pulled to the North Pole by magnetism.

Look at these pictures. Circle 7 things that are different in the picture above.

What's for Lunch?

The school cafeteria is very busy today. Henry Herbivore only eats plants. Carl Carnivore only eats meat. Omar Omnivore eats plants and meat.

Look at these pictures. Circle 7 things that are different in the picture above.

In the Garden

Animals *do* more than just eat plants. Some animals help plants by moving pollen from one plant to another or scattering their seeds.

Look at these pictures. Circle 8 things that are different in the picture above.

The Power of Water

Water can change landscapes by moving rock and soil from one area to another.
This is called erosion. The Grand Canyon was created by erosion.

Look at these pictures. Circle 7 things that are different in the picture above.

Black Sand

When lava reaches the sea, it cools rapidly. This causes the volcanic material to shatter into black sand. The sand collects on the shore, forming black sand beaches.

Look at these pictures. Circle 8 things that are different in the picture above.

Thank You, Mr. Edison

As you listen to music, turn on a light, or watch a movie today, think of Thomas Edison. He invented the phonograph, the lightbulb, and the movie camera.

Look at these pictures. Circle 7 things that are different in the picture above.

On the Moon

Weight is caused by the force of gravity. A 100-lb. barbell on Earth only weighs 16.6 lbs. on the moon. Why? Because the moon's gravitational force is less than Earth's.

Look at these pictures. Circle 7 things that are different in the picture above.

Changing Geography

The Hoover Dam was built on the Colorado River in 1936. This changed the physical geography of the area. It flooded the area above the dam and created Lake Mead.

Look at these pictures. Circle 7 things that are different in the picture above.

Life on the Plains

Buffalo were very important to the Plains Indians of North America. They were used for food, clothing, shelter, tools, blankets, and more. Nothing was wasted.

Look at these pictures. Circle 7 things that are different in the picture above.

Totem Poles

Native Americans along the Pacific Northwest coast carved totem poles from tall trees. The poles used animals to tell stories about the past.

Look at these pictures. Circle 7 things that are different in the picture above.

Stars and Stripes

Betsy Ross made the first American flag in 1776. It had 13 stars and 13 stripes because there were 13 colonies. Now it has 50 stars representing the 50 states.

Look at these pictures. Circle 7 things that are different in the picture above.

Lewis and Clark

With the help of Sacajawea, Lewis and Clark explored the area between the Mississippi River and the Pacific Ocean from 1804-1806. Their maps helped people move west.

Look at these pictures. Circle 7 things that are different in the picture above.

Order in the Court!

In the United States, a person accused of a crime has the right to a jury trial. A jury is a group of citizens who listen to the facts and decide if the person is guilty or innocent.

Look at these pictures. Circle 7 things that are different in the picture above.

The Right to Vote

Susan B. Anthony was part of the women's suffrage movement, which fought for the right of women to vote in the United States. Women won the right to vote in 1920.

Look at these pictures. Circle 7 things that are different in the picture above.

Hot New Toy!

When a lot of people buy a new toy, they create a demand for it. The toy maker then increases the supply (the number of toys it makes) to meet the demand.

Look at these pictures. Circle 7 things that are different in the picture above.

Maps, Maps, and More Maps

Maps do more than show how to get someplace. They can show geographic features, resources, weather, boundaries, and elevation.

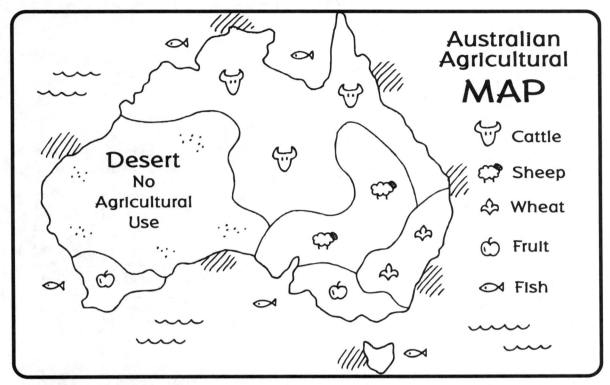

Look at these pictures. Circle 7 things that are different in the picture above.

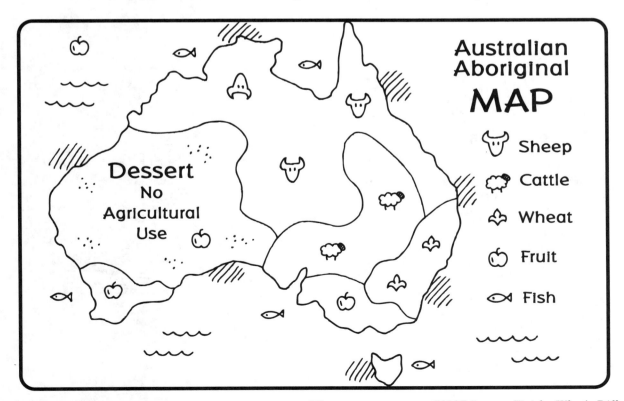

California Missions

Beginning in 1769, Spanish Catholics built and ran 21 missions in what is now California. They wanted to make the Native Americans citizens of Spain as well as Christians.

Look at these pictures. Circle 7 things that are different in the picture above.

28   ©Teacher Created Resources

Gold Rush

Gold was found in California in 1848. People from around the world came by ship and covered wagon. They all wanted to strike it rich, but very few did.

Look at these pictures. Circle 8 things that are different in the picture above.

The Model T

Henry Ford built the Model T on an assembly line. Priced at a little over $800 in 1909, it was the first car that the average person could afford to buy.

Look at these pictures. Circle 8 things that are different in the picture above.

Hail to the Chief

The U.S. Constitution states that to be president, a person must be a natural-born citizen, at least 35 years old, and a resident for at least 14 years.

Look at these pictures. Circle 8 things that are different in the picture above.

Climbing Everest

Mt. Everest is the tallest mountain in the world (29,029 feet). Extreme altitude, weather, and wind make it very dangerous, but brave adventurers attempt to climb it every year.

Look at these pictures. Circle 8 things that are different in the picture above.

32 ©Teacher Created Resources

Dozens of Donuts

When does a dozen equal 13? When it's a baker's dozen! If you ask for a dozen eggs, you'll get 12. If you ask for a dozen donuts, you'll often get 13, a baker's dozen.

Look at these pictures. Circle 8 things that are different in the picture above.

33

It Weighs a Ton!

A ton is 2,000 pounds. A small car weighs about a ton. A bull walrus weighs about two tons. A bull African elephant, the largest land animal, weighs about six tons.

Look at these pictures. Circle 8 things that are different in the picture above.

The Super Shape

Engineers and architects often use triangles in constructing buildings and
bridges because triangles are very stable and strong.

Look at these pictures. Circle 8 things that are different in the picture above.

Let's Get Cooking!

It is important to measure the volume of ingredients with the right tools. Use a dry measuring cup for dry ingredients and a liquid measuring cup for wet ingredients.

Look at these pictures. Circle 8 things that are different in the picture above.

Heads or Tails?

Why is a coin flip fair? There is a 50% chance that it will be heads and a 50% chance that it will be tails. The probability is the same for both heads and tails.

Look at these pictures. Circle 8 things that are different in the picture above.

Six Figures

Six figures refers to the amount of money someone earns or how much
something costs. There are six figures in the amount, making it hundreds of
thousands of dollars.

Look at these pictures. Circle 9 things that are different in the picture above.

 ©*Teacher Created Resources*

On Track

Train tracks are made of parallel lines. The New York City subway system uses about 660 miles of parallel lines, or track, to transport millions of people daily.

Look at these pictures. Circle 8 things that are different in the picture above.

Swoosh!

The diameter of a basketball hoop is 18 inches. But what is the radius? The diameter of a circle is 2 times the radius. Therefore, we know that the radius is 9 inches.

Look at these pictures. Circle 8 things that are different in the picture above.

Big Hitter

Batting averages are calculated by dividing the number of hits by the number of at bats. Ty Cobb holds the record with a career average of .366. He played from 1905–1928.

Look at these pictures. Circle 9 things that are different in the picture above.

Get Your Hot Dogs!

Lucy, Jack, and Will entered a hot dog eating contest. Lucy ate 5 ½ hot dogs. Jack ate 5.5 hot dogs. Will ate 5 hot dogs and 50% of another. Who won? It was a tie!

Look at these pictures. Circle 8 things that are different in the picture above.

What's Going to Happen?

The witch in "Hansel and Gretel" fattens up the children, giving us a clue to what she plans to do with them . . . eat them! This type of clue is called *foreshadowing*.

Look at these pictures. Circle 8 things that are different in the picture above.

Aesop's Fables

Aesop was a slave and storyteller in Greece about 2,500 years ago. His fables, such as "The Tortoise and the Hare," taught people about how they should act.

Look at these pictures. Circle 8 things that are different in the picture above.

Picture This!

Good writers paint a picture for the reader using descriptive, sensory words. For example, "Smelly socks, crumpled papers, and old pizza boxes littered the room."

Look at these pictures. Circle 8 things that are different in the picture above.

Tongue-Tied

Tongue twisters use alliteration (the same consonant at the beginning of several words in a row) and rhyme to make them tricky to say, especially fast!

Seven silly swans swam silently seaward.

Look at these pictures. Circle 8 things that are different in the picture above.

Seven silly swans swam sliently seaward

A Spider and a Pig

Charlotte's Web, which was first published in 1952, is one of the best-selling children's books of all time. It is one of only three children's books written by E.B. White.

Look at these pictures. Circle 8 things that are different in the picture above.

Idioms

An idiom is a saying that means something different. For example, "raining cats and dogs" does not mean it is really raining cats and dogs. It means it is raining very hard.

Look at these pictures. Circle 9 things that are different in the picture above.

The Newbery Medal

Looking for a good book? Check out a Newbery Medal winner. Since 1922, this annual award has been given to the author of the best children's book of the year.

Look at these pictures. Circle 8 things that are different in the picture above.

Stick to the Script

Actors memorize their lines before performing on television or in movies. The script tells the actors who is in each scene and what their lines are.

Look at these pictures. Circle 8 things that are different in the picture above.

Little House on the Prairie

The Little House series of books is an example of historical fiction. It is based on the life of the author, Laura Ingalls Wilder, but it combines historical facts with fiction.

Look at these pictures. Circle 8 things that are different in the picture above.

Buy This!

Food and drink companies spend over 1.5 billion dollars every year to make you want to buy their products. Before buying, ask yourself "Is this really a good choice for me?"

Look at these pictures. Circle 8 things that are different in the picture above.

Hold Still

A painting, drawing, or photograph of a nonliving object or group of objects is called a still life. Flower arrangements and fruit are often used as subject matter.

Look at these pictures. Circle 8 things that are different in the picture above.

Mona Lisa's Missing!

Leonardo da Vinci's *Mona Lisa* was stolen from the Louvre Museum in Paris in 1911. Luckily, it was found two years later. It is one of the world's most famous paintings.

Look at these pictures. Circle 8 things that are different in the picture above.

Full of Air

The tuba is the largest brass instrument. It plays the lowest notes. Brass instruments produce sound as the musician's lips vibrate as he or she blows into the mouthpiece.

Look at these pictures. Circle 8 things that are different in the picture above.

It Takes Four

A string quartet is a group of four musicians who play string instruments (two violins, a viola, and a cello). Usually, they play classical music for small audiences.

Look at these pictures. Circle 8 things that are different in the picture above.

Take a Look

Public art is made to be displayed in an area where everyone can enjoy it. Because it is often displayed outside, sculpture is a popular medium due to its durability.

Look at these pictures. Circle 8 things that are different in the picture above.

Answer Key

Page 4

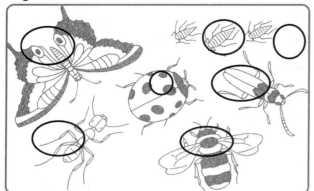

Page 5

Page 6

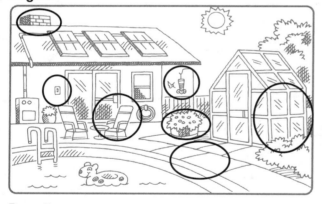

Page 7

Page 8

Page 9

Page 10

Page 11

Answer Key *(cont.)*

Page 12

Page 13

Page 14

Page 15

Page 16

Page 17

Page 18

Page 19

Answer Key *(cont.)*

Page 20

Page 21

Page 22

Page 23

Page 24

Page 25

Page 26

Page 27

Answer Key *(cont.)*

Page 28

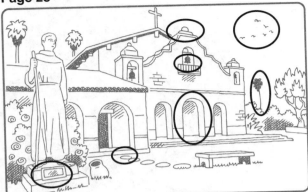

Page 32

Page 29

Page 33

Page 30

Page 34

Page 31

Page 35

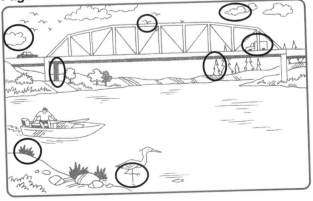

Answer Key (cont.)

Page 36

Page 37

Page 38

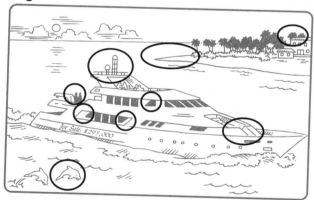

Page 39

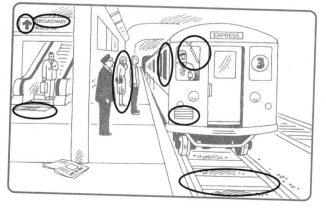

Page 40

Page 41

Page 42

Page 43

Answer Key *(cont.)*

Page 44

Page 45

Page 46

Page 47

Page 48

Page 49

Page 50

Page 51

Answer Key (cont.)

Page 52

Page 53

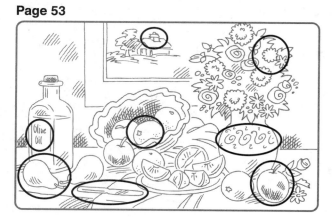

Page 54

Page 55

Page 56

Page 57